I FOR AN I

AN EPISTOLARY COLLECTION

SWARNIKA

ISBN 979-888591718-6

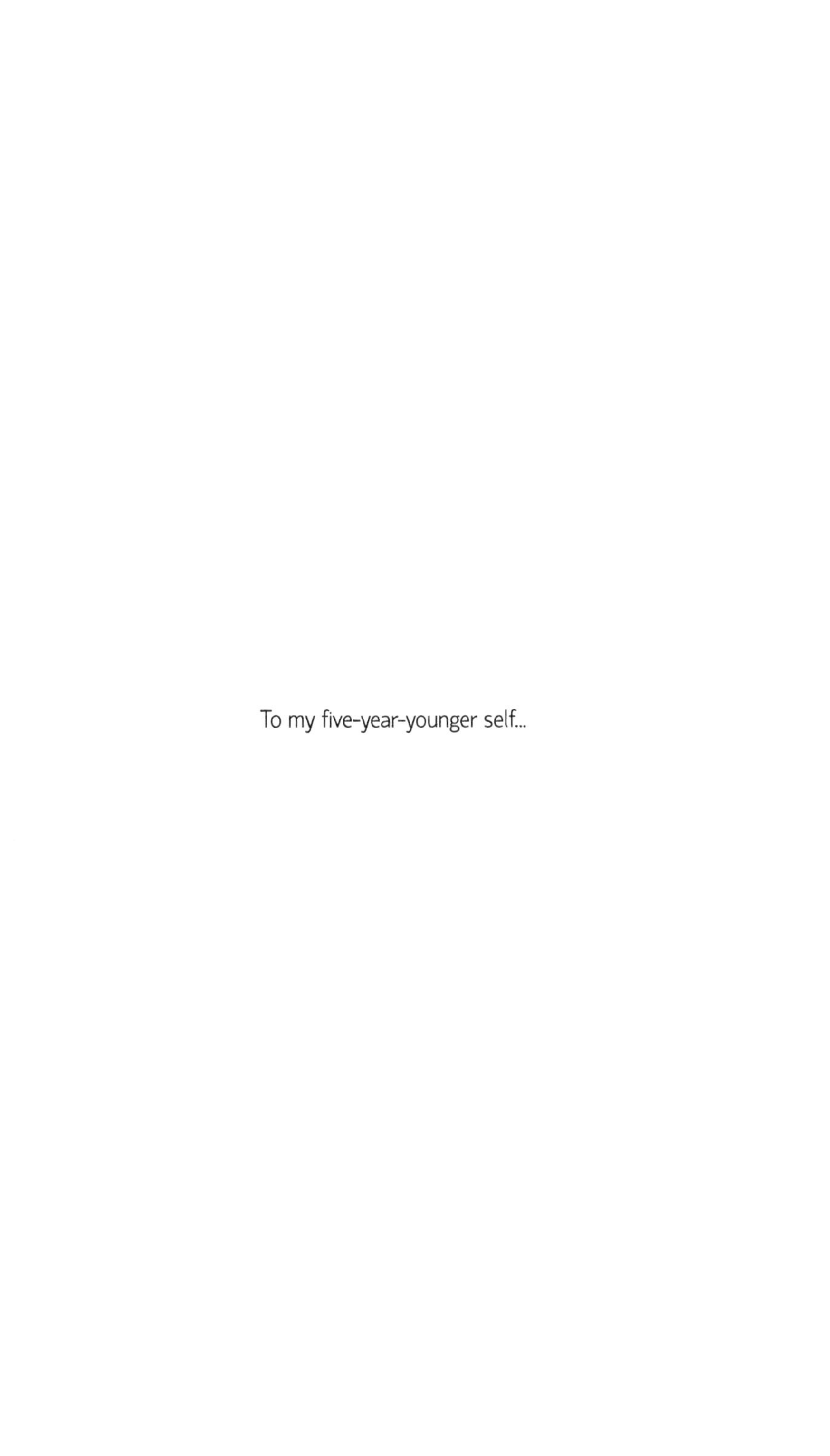
To my five-year-younger self...

Contents

Foreword

Letter, Khat, Sandesa, Or Chithi; not only do these Hindi words become obsolete with time, but the activity of writing letters too has become such an archaic practice that it seems to be like some other planet's exercise, far away from the present. My maternal grandfather was a head postmaster, So my relationship with letters is quite special. I once asked him, casually, Don't you feel inferior with such a meagre job, you could have become something else, some elite profession? Though he chose to become postman because of economic and family pressures, then promoted to head postmaster after a long period of time, it was difficult for him initially, especially traveling on foot, (bicycles only came later), and that too long miles away. I remember his answer till now not because it was too long, but it changed me right at the moment and I literally wish I can travel back to the time when every house jubilantly dances on the gleeful cry of "Chithi aayi hai". He said that letters are not only a means of communication in the era of without mobile phones and video calls, it is some other kind of cheerfulness which not only the reader of the letter enjoys but the whole family gathers in unity to read a letter from a distant relative. "Chithi aayi hai" (a letter has come), this joyful cry, a jouissance, where the whole house awakens from a long sleep is something which motivated him to continue his profession, to bring happiness at every door where his bicycle can reach. It was a ritual at that time to give sweets to the postman for harbinging good news and if it was bad news, the demise of dear ones, to see them in tears is most hurtful because implicitly the postman is the reason. So the job was not difficult for crossing distant miles but to bear the pain of others' misery.

This present compendium of letters is not sent to unknown persons or strangers, they are sent to the old selves of each person, letters written to five year-older selves. In a period when we can cross temporal barriers for communicating our dear ones through phone and video calls, and holograms are anticipating the technological future, we can communicate with them anytime, literally. This collection brings a backward turnover to the time in two levels, firstly, reviving the old spirit of letter writing and secondly, to the past, to our own old self. Oftenly, I wish sometimes dejectedly, if really five years back, a knock at my door brought a letter from my future self, just to say "You will be Okay". But that was meant to not happen, not because it is an illogical fantasy, practically not possible but because if I read that letter from my future self at that moment, I wouldn't be able to cross that river of misery and become this, which I am today, able to stand on my feet. There is a wise saying which my mother once said, to become a diamond from coal, one has to burn. So, that burning, suffering was necessary for me, it was part of my development, and so many others who have contributed to this collection.

Hoilalnei Hmar poignantly pens down her journey of survival from virulent jeers from the society which unabashedly measures her in conventional scales of womanhood, but she resisted for being judged by someone else. While Gauri Shukla's renewed version pens down an inducing note of her roller coaster life saga, from tackling personal problems to professional life, she excels gracefully in each struggle of her life. What can I say for Pooja or Putul, she wrote a light-hearted e-mail to her five year older self, since she believed at least e-mail has the possibility of reaching the past, and why not? Now comes Khushi Kaushik whose succinct letter says a lot of things which are so common in all our lives. Similarly, Raman too laid bare his life on blank paper to console his older version. Deepanshi and Nishtha unveils their past to reconcile the balance between past and present.

Deepanshi Ailawadi

Preface

I for an I is an epistolary anthology that consists of letters by the writers addressed to their five-year younger selves. There is a lot that we wish we could say or do to ourselves when we were younger. We do this in the hope that maybe we might have done things differently and have led ourselves to a better life at this point in life. Penning these thoughts down sometimes helps us resonate better with our current situations and work towards a better future. The following anthology is just a collection of these thoughts. maybe some reader would be able to relate to someone's letter or part from it as well. Maybe it will help them. We never know when something might end up creating an impact on our life. Maybe it will help us, the writers, when we are stuck somewhere or are close to giving up. The possibilities could create another universe.

Swarnika

Director-Mentor
Nrityangana Kala Kendra

Acknowledgements

Working on this collection has been a wonderful experience, but it wouldn't have been the same without the dedication and contributions made by my fellow writers. All of them have exhibited initiative as well as pertinence.

I'd like to thank Gauri Shukla, Khushi Kaushik, Putul Mangni Mandal, Raman Singh, Deepanshi Ailawadi, Nishtha Trehan, and Hoilalnei Hmar for working on the letters present in this collection and sharing them with our readers. They have not just shared these letters, but have also shared a part of themselves, a part of their stories.

Prologue

Dear Reader,

While you embark on this journey reading the letters by the writers of this anthology, we hope that you can resonate, associate, and correlate. We understand that you might have a lot to say to your younger selves. We all hope things could be better today if you did certain things differently. But let me tell you that you're doing so well. You don't have to be like anyone else. You're being the best version of yourself. Keep working on your personal growth.

You should be proud of all that you've accomplished and all that you've been through. You have made it through. Yes, you still have a long way to go. After all, the sky is the limit, right?

Maybe you'll end up writing your own letter to your younger self and it might end up helping you or someone else. You never know what might be in store for you in the future.

Happy Reading!

Wishing you all the best,

Swarnika

Swarnika

Swarnika is an avid reader and an ambivert. She is a glass-half-full kind of a person, not because she is always an optimist but because she believes that a glass that is full has no more scope and ends up creating the most amount of spills.

She completed her Bachelor's and Master's degree from the University of Delhi. She has completed her three-level professional certification in Spanish from Valencia Polytechnic University, Spain. She has also completed her certificate program in French from St. Stephen's College, University of Delhi. She is currently pursuing a Post-Graduate Diploma in Business Administration from Symbiosis Centre for Distance Learning, Pune. She is working on her thesis and research papers to earn her Ph.D. degree in English Literature.

She has a keen interest in criminology and detective fiction. Writings that indulge mystery and rationale speak volumes to her. She has earned her TEFL and TESOL certificates as an English language teacher. She is also a certified dance teacher with specializations in Bharatnatyam, Kathak, and Contemporary. She is also certified in Classical Music and Fine Arts.

She exhibits abundant admiration for food and would call herself a foodie. She believes in living in the moment rather than giving the moment the opportunity to live through you without you even realizing it. She has started her company- Nrityangana Kala Kendra OPC Private Limited on her own. She has been tutoring kids along with mentoring graduate and postgraduate students in academic and creative writing.

On some days she is a dreamer while on others she is a realist. She firmly believes in humanism. Nature mesmerizes her. On a usual day, you'd find her curled up in a corner either with a book or watching a movie/ episode while relishing food.

She has initiated this project and has edited the book along with compiling it.

CHAPTER ONE

Letter 1

Dear Swara,

You're going to be alright.

Anything would become impossible to accomplish once you give up on it. The key to success is to be adamant, persistent, and consistent. You and you alone, are the only permanent thing in your life.

I know this must sound like a segment from a pep-talk but you need to realize how important this is for you. You've just turned eighteen and you feel you're ready to embrace the world as it is. I know you are. In fact, let me tell you something, you're prepared for things you never thought you'd be. You have potential that you yourself don't realize. You'll break apart some days but never shatter beyond repair. You'll mend yourself into something even more beautiful, something even stronger than before. You'll be growing wiser and kinder every single day. And when you feel like giving up, just remember that it is you who is going to decide what your future is going to look like. Nobody, let me say this with emphasis, NOBODY can give you better advice than what you can seek for yourself. Nobody has the right to make those decisions for you, whosoever it may be. Take this from your own, a little older and a little wiser, self.

I'll be honest with you. Sometimes I do wish I could be eighteen again and do a few things differently. Maybe I'd be able to avoid certain mistakes. Maybe I can walk away from those who're just looking for trouble. Maybe I'd be able to utilize my time better and make better decisions. Maybe I could achieve the things I have been achieving a little early. Maybe I wouldn't waste time on people who don't deserve a second of it. Maybe I won't let people influence my life. Maybe I won't let my parents control my life for the most part of it. Trust me; you have done so much better when you've just listened to your heart. This is from experience that I'm telling you that what you do is the best for you. Nobody else knows this. They can assume and presume but they can never comprehend it.

You are smart enough to know what is right and what is not. Don't let people and situations intimidate you. You are a kind soul. You can't hurt people the way they do. There is nothing wrong with that. There is nothing wrong with being a decent human out there. People might make you doubt that sometimes but don't let them change you. You are fine. You are good. You are beautiful. You are kind. You care. Don't feel weird about caring for people who have been mean to you or haven't done right by you. Their actions and choices are the reflection of their personality. What you do is the reflection of your character. You are this person. And you don't have to change that for anyone. You have a comprehensive soul. It is beautiful how you don't just act upon everything and would take a while to first understand the other person's point of view and then evaluate the situation. That just shows that you do respect yourself and try to understand others. You don't just insult others, and by that yourself, by just speaking hurtful things. There is a difference between being straightforward and being a jerk. You know that and that's good. For some people, it takes up years of their life to understand this. Some would continue doing wrong by others, even though they are fully aware that they can't justify their words and actions.

Prioritize yourself. Don't expect anyone else to do it. Let me put it across you- no one is going to. You decide your fate. You should be your own priority. You shouldn't need anyone in your life. Yes, be kind and respect others the way you'd want to be respected. After all, you get what you give. People are temporary. Even the people closest to you can't always be there for you and that is okay. You needn't hold it against them or doubt yourself. You need to be there for yourself and shouldn't need anything more than that. Yes, it would be nice to hang out with friends sometimes and maybe have a nice family dinner. But even without these; you should be able to find your happiness, your peace. You should be at peace with yourself. If you aren't then it should be your priority to find it.

You would achieve everything you'd want once you put your heart and soul into it. Don't give up. You are more capable than you sometimes think you are. Stop doubting yourself and trust your instincts. Your instincts are a gift. You are very intuitive. It helps you perceive and evaluate a lot. Let it aid your self-growth. Do right by yourself. People doing wrong by you would seem inconsequential. They won't matter. Anyone who'd take advantage of the goodness in the heart of another, anyway, doesn't deserve to stay in mind or heart.

It is good that you like to explore. You'd take up multiple things altogether and try to do well in them. There are going to be people who'd have a lot to say about it. You might have an idea about who I'm talking about. Just multiply the list tenfold and you'd know how many people are going to speak against your choices. Now I'm not going to tell you who you should trust and who you should avoid. I believe that being able to comprehend it on your own and make decisions for yourself is a process that you should undertake now only. It would make you wiser and more understanding at the same time. Don't let them get to your head. Don't believe it when they tell you that you can't have it all. They'd tell you that trying to have it all; you'll end up screwing everything. Just show them how to ace it. That is all you need. After all, actions and results speak volumes. And from I to another I, you have done justice to the motto. There is still a lot that you're doing but a lot you've already done.

> "*A jack of trades is a master of none; but is still better than the master of one.*"

Might I say when I look back at our journey, I feel proud of the growth. You'll be too someday. So whenever you feel like giving up or giving into someone else's opinion, just remember that your future is bright but only if it's you who lead the path. Others intervening would only deviate you from your goals. Maybe you'd read this. Maybe you'll take these into account. Maybe you'll do better and do even better in life. I'll wish you all the best; I want to give you a lot of love and strength. You would really need it. Don't be spooked. As I said, you are stronger than you know. You'd get a lot but for that, you might have to go through a lot. You weren't born with a silver spoon in your mouth. People might not always have the best of their intentions towards you. You might not have a wonderful environment around you but then not every place is the Garden of Eden. You'll get by. You'll make the most of every situation.

Don't discontinue dance and music. Keep pursuing it. It would bring so much peace to your soul when everything else is chaotic. Don't depend on anyone to pay your bills. Do internships. Take up part-time jobs. Even go for something permanent later. Take up projects. Continue writing. Explore different genres. You'd be getting published one day. Read more. You have enough books today to have a huge library. Learn more. Work on your skills. Get a lot more of them in your bag. Take up courses and workshops. Go for seminars and present papers. Take up research projects on your own and keep working on them. Don't discard your writings. Don't leave them halfway. Finish it, even if you think it is not good enough. Once you finish it, keep working on it. Keep revising it. Learn languages. You know French and Spanish right now. You're learning Korean and might take up another language soon. So keep learning. The day you decide that you've learned a lot and might stop now, is the day you would stop growing. Every day is a new opportunity to learn. And when you'd learn about different languages, you'll become inquisitive about different cultures. You'll learn so much more about different nations, cultures and their people. Don't stop watching movies or series just because some would opine that it is a waste of time. It is not. You learn a lot from them as well. Watch movies from different cultures and on different themes. Watch documentaries. Watch movies in different languages. Even when you watch them with subtitles, you learn the language slowly. Listen to music in these languages. Do the things that you want to do and let them be the source of your growth. As much you appreciate the foreign culture, appreciate the one you inherited here, in India. Ancient Tamil and Sanskrit literature is as exquisite as is the ruins in Athens and the works of Homer.

I can't emphasize enough but work on your growth. Personal growth should be your priority. Don't seek happiness in places or in people. Your happiness lies within you. Don't be scared. Be fearless. You know what is right for you. Go for it. If it was right, you get what you wanted. Sometimes, even more. If not, you learn a lesson. You gain experience. So keep taking a chance. Keep taking a chance on yourself. And don't let anyone take your advantage. You don't have any rights over anyone's money so you should make it on your own. What you own and earn is yours. What belongs to someone else is theirs. Remember this. By this, I would also like to point out that don't let anyone take your monetary worth or growth for granted. Don't let anyone drain you emotionally. Don't give anyone that much power over yourself. You are nice and kind but don't let that turn against you. Know your worth and know what is going to hurt you. Learn to be nice and kind to yourself.

With that, I'll leave you to your thoughts. Trust yourself. I am sending a lot of love and strength to you via some time machine. Spend your time and money on yourself. You're worth it.

Know you're loved.

With admiration and hope,

Swarnika

A little older and a little wiser version of you.

Deepanshi Ailawadi

Deepanshi Ailawadi holds a Master's degree in English Literature. Since childhood libraries are her second home which enables her to travel across time and space. She believes each written page tells a story that should not be left unheard because in the end human beings are made up of little stories stored up in their brain's memory. Writing is one of the mediums through which stories can be heard, touched, and felt. Thus, she decided to write, to pay back her debt to Reading and disseminate stories that have the capability to reform our ways of perception. Writing enables her to hold several personalities and perspectives in her body, sometimes she becomes a bookseller, while other times she becomes a buyer of the book, and sometimes she can be both friend and enemy at once. It is this magic that tempted her to write for others and for herself too.

CHAPTER TWO

Letter 2

Dear Deepanshi,

I hope you are doing well and have been continuously crossing hindrances on your way. So do not let yourself down and keep the faith. You will not believe what the future has stored for you. I know you are a little disappointed about not getting admitted to BCA, but the course that you have been admitted to will change your life enormously. After five years, you will realise that you were made for this course because it will let you express yourself efficiently and make you understand that, apart from your love, there lies a huge world. "Understanding other people's stories makes you more human," they say. You will definitely notice it when you begin to read the newspaper. Remember, after your trivial breakup, each piece of news strikes you back violently, whether it is about rape, migration, violence, or whatnot. When Faiz laments, "aur bhi gham hain zamane mein, vasl ki chahto ke siwa," I never understand how anything can be more tragic than personal loss, but this is exactly what stories do, eventually shifting your position to another's to make you understand another's miseries. Nevertheless, I know there are other disappointments too: not-so-good college, relationship problems, and family issues. But without hardships, life is nothing, as the wise saying claims, and you must have heard the song "zindagi ki yahi reet hai, har me baad hi jeet hai"

You've been afraid of losing since childhood, from a loved one to your favourite hair clip, but eventually, you'll realise it's important to embrace the loss. Everybody will tell you to suffer in pain, but as I am a result of yours, I will just say to keep your pace and handle them in your own way. Obviously, you will be hurt, and you will fall from your high expectations of life, but this is necessary unless you are afraid of making decisions at every point in life. I won't tell you about the future, but I will tell you about the types of people you will meet in the near future. As usual, you will make friends who will become part of your life for a while and leave you soon. For your relationship, you will be submerged deeper into that ocean, and when you come back, you will become me. I know it is a difficult phase of your life, but sooner or later you will laugh at your little worries, as you have done in the past, as I laugh. Do not think that I am laughing at you; I am only thinking about how naive and childish I was, and still am. There is some corner in my heart that longs for my lost nativity. As for now, I am still not very mature to give advice because there is more to learn from life for me in the future. This is the key to life; just keep learning.

I know you have adult suicidal tendencies too. You have already written your death note, and I will not stop you, but these five years will teach you that not every solution comes from death. Open your newspaper one day and read how many homeless people survive without shelter, how many unlucky soldiers returning from their regiments to their homes die unnoticed, or simply go outside your house and see how street hawkers dressed in sweaters and mufflers sell in bitter cold for a few rupees.

You have to be strong, not like a tree's bark but like a hurricane, so whenever time comes, you can transform into a serene ocean.If someone is trying to find the exit gates from your life, then help them. Do not become an obstacle in their way. You can't keep them in your fist for very long.Just let them go. In a few minutes new people will arrive in your life. I know no one can replace any person, but you have to acknowledge life's rules: from one gate, someone will go, but from the other window, somebody will come too. The only thing is that you do not fix your eyes on that closed gate, but look at the little windows too.

Most importantly, stop thinking too much. Invest your time in some meaningful work. This advice is still valid for me because I am also doing the same. I know you cannot prevent yourself from worrying about the future, and that is why I am suggesting you apply for some extracurricular activities and open yourself to the outside world. Fear is not a solution, and how many things or how many people do you fear? Your parents, teachers, friends, siblings, shopkeepers, watchmen, you are afraid of every stranger in your life. Do not let your fear press you so hard that you can never be reborn. I know your fear is not your weakness but only concern for others, but trust me, you never hurt anybody, and if you did so, your guilt has always been with you to realize. Have you heard the modern adage, "You can't be chocolate and make everyone happy."? So, just remember to not make your life more complicated because these five years taught me that it is only our individual efforts that decide our happiness.

I am not suggesting you accept your drawbacks, but work upon them. I know you're worried about being mocked, but don't even think about it. They are not part of your dream. Remember that for your impossible dreams, people will crush you down on every step, but you have to hold yourself up. They will also leave your life like your loved ones, but it is only up to you whom you will keep in your heart. Keep them saying that and move forward on your path.

If you ever lose something, assume that it will come back to you after some period of time. If you fail any examination, assume that some other guy needed to pass it more than you, or you are not yet ready to pass the examination, so begin your preparation again. Do you remember your small kari patta plant? It is now so tall that you wouldn't believe it. Its bark is still the same, only its roots are thick and strong. During autumn, leaves fall so drastically that you almost cry. During heavy storms, it quivered tragically, and I thought I would never see it, but the next morning it surprised me, standing high in straight stature. During these five years, it taught me to be slow in learning, in suffering, and in enjoying, because turning life into slow motion enhances its taste.

Nature is a slow teacher, but an effective one.

Today, I think if this letter knocked on your door somehow, I would not feel lonely in my life. In those five years, I felt that no one was ever born unlucky like me. There was no one with whom I could talk, no one with whom I could share my dilemma. However, sometimes burning in a fire is as important as lighting the room. I wonder if I had not gone through that period of life, I would never get away from my fear of loss. You know, I lost my PhD examination. My NET experience was horrible, but I am not disappointed because I now understand the intricacies of incidents.

What is lost is lost; just rebuild that broken step and try again to ascend the ladder. For a while, I was broken, but my over-thinking helped me speculate on why this failure occurred. My heart consoled me by saying "don't cry right now" because people understand failure's reason only in the future. You will soon understand why you were not admitted to BCA, so that you can opt for English honors. You did not get into a reputed college because in your destiny you had to meet Disha ma'am. You did not get admitted to regular MA English because your mother needed you more than the classroom of any good college. You did not join any NGO because you needed to spend some memorable moments with your love before you separated. There is always a reason behind the events of our lives, but we only understand them later. So, just keep calm and be happy, because life is all about suffering, as Buddha said, but you have to find happiness in the midst of darkness.

Lastly, I want to reiterate my previous advice: just do not let your fear consume you. Concern for others is good, but only to its limit. Whenever things move in an extreme direction, history has witnessed a person's fall. Whenever you try hard to achieve something and consequently arrive at a failure, just say to your heart to try harder and then hardest. Never be afraid to put in the effort. Whatever the outcome, remember that trees shed thousands of leaves every year, but they never stop growing higher and higher. With this last note, I will end this letter and hope that you will burry your fears in a deep pit. What is more, yes, it is equally important to thank those people who made this letter possible for me to write. They say no one can understand your problems better than you, Truly said.

Deepanshi

From a slightly wiser and older you.

Putul Mangni Mandal

Living in New Delhi, Putul Mangni Mandal was born in December 1996. It is a pseudonym that she has adopted for the literary world. By root, her family comes from Bihar and as mentioned in the name, she belongs to the Mandal community. However, she abhors rigid statism or communism. Putul (meaning doll; it is her mother's pet name) lives with her small family of four. Financially, she is lower middle class. She studied in a government school named Sarvodaya Co. Ed. Senior Secondary in Nanak Pura. She has done her Post Graduation in English from Delhi University and aspires to become a professional writer, too, among many other possible-impossible things.

Poems have fascinated her ever since she read Kanyadān, a poem by the famous romantic Hindi writer Suryakānt Tripāthi 'Nirālā' in tenth grade. But she never knew that she could write until the day when her teacher Minākshi Mehta asked the whole class to create something. She composed her first poem Lakshya. Since then she has written many poems. Some of her English poems include On a Bus, Chores, Substitute, My Days, At Last, A Signal, and many others. She also writes in Hindi/Urdu and some of them are Intezār, Ūpar-Neechey, Bheetar, Chāl, etc. Fingers crossed, she hopes to soon come up with her poem collection. Not limiting herself to poems only, she has initiated in the field of prose writing through her first work Listen Didi which is a novella. Apart from this she also likes to write articles and essays on various literary topics.

She hopes that people will find something interesting and unique in her work. If they do so, they may use her email address given below to express their useful views.

Putulmangnimandal@gmail.com

CHAPTER THREE

Letter 3

Dear Pooja,

May nature grace you with more strength to fight the psychological chaos you will experience a couple of years from now. How do I know your future, you ask? Well, this is me—your five-year-old self. You must be really flushed right now. Don't worry, love; you're seeing glimpses of what was once only a theory — time travel!

Look, I don't exactly understand the technicalities of this science stuff, but if this email finds you successfully, it simply proves that humans have at least reached the rope to time travel. No, we still aren't able to. Send humans back to the past because it will surely take at least a decade more, but we can send messages, if that matters, to our past selves via the internet. Who knew the hidden marvels of American magic? Hey, You must call me Didi. That's the least I expect from you. Hungry for respect. Aren't we all! By the way, I am here for a serious reason. The world is about to face an unprecedented pandemic and you need to save the world... I got you! You're such a movie geek! I know you've been watching so many American movies, so I took a tiny advantage of my advanced position. The world will have to face a pandemic called COVID-19 though, but you can't really control the future. Can you? No one could! So just be yourself and let things happen. I am here to appreciate your efforts in constituting me, your future self, and preparing you for certain things that will come abruptly and a HELL NO if you're expecting me to reveal what your future pertains to. Why would someone ask for a movie spoiler? Please embrace all the disappointments of life with open arms as you do with success.

I know that you've just broken up with your boyfriend and the days are filled with guilt for hurting his innocent heart, but trust me, babe, you have made the right decision! Don't be confused only because the world is pointing a finger at your decision. A tiny repressed corner of your heart had been protesting against your decision ever since you began that relationship. Don't deny it now, please. You are not a cruel person by any means. You have an equal right to not fall in love with a person. Bollywood is of fungal spores that have infected drenching young brains but you must save yourself. He'll be fine, I can assure you of that. Hey, why don't you replace your regrets with respect? I don't mean to suggest a complete exclusion of regret because it needs to be there in a small size, but spawn it if you've got a great amount of respect exchanged. How can you do that? It ain't no rocket science. Delicate oysters make solid pearls, so try to find your pearls in sensitive situations. You simply start to accept the thing you regret, saying it again— embrace disappointments. You start to care about yourself or the other person/s, if you have any regretful actions related to your concern, Then you try to compensate for it. Like in your current case, you have no control over your ex-boyfriend's future actions, nor do you have any over your already done actions. But what you can do now is to look at the good part. You must be saying, "oh, I know it already, tell me something new," but DO YOU REALLY? Were you really this self-aware before it happened? Did you not improve your writing skills by making tonnes of poems about the situation that you now call REGRET? Are you not grateful for his kindness and respect? I mean, in the parallel world, he could be a mean person. You know you respect him, so keep on doing it. Love him for his honest love and let him go. No "at-least-friend"! You can't keep him. It would do no good to either of you. So chill. You already have enough anxiety over such a trivial issue. Focus on yourself now, on your career, and on your friends.

In terms of your professional life... you are not worried about your career as much, Are you? Well, what can I say? It's not your time to worry so much about it. You are only twenty. See, I will be twenty-five in a few weeks and I still don't have a proper job. You're in a good time when Papa still has a job. You never know when a private job will slip through your fingers and you'll be crying about your dwindling savings. I understand you don't want to be entangled in pity jobs, and I agree with you. You must save your time and study more. But, in the meantime, remember not to lose touch with your family. When bad times come, we often blame others for being negligent or even bringing bad luck. It creates two things in a sequence — chaos, followed by silence. It becomes difficult to live inside a house that has either of these. What you are left with is hard work, optimistic hope, and support. Be the glue of your family. You have already found the best of the best friends— Pratibha, how grateful you must be. She'll stand by your side during rough times. You're also going to make really good friends. Some of them will be superficial, but a lot of them will resonate with your soul. You must not lose them. You have a bad habit of not asking about their health and well-being. You think you know they're fine, , but no, it's not true. Many people love the things that you'd abhor personally. So, make yourself flexible so that they can adjust with you. Notice them like you notice yourself in the mirror and be helpful. And please never expect anything in return.

Okay! I know you already do. Still, just in case. I'm still the same. Mostly, everyone is talking about the rage of the pandemic, but death and disease are not new. You will have to face a death in the house way back before the pandemic begins. Just be assured that it's not your immediate family and you'll not only do fine but also take it with responsibility. Still, I need to share something. It is not a useful lesson, as you might expect from your future self.

See, this is exactly what I meant to tell you. When someone important dies unexpectedly, we try to return to the past and relive it so that we can spend more time with them, respect them more, love them more, accept their circumstances, and never fight. It seems like a chance to relish the person one last time PROPERLY. But I say, there is no such thing as "proper." A decent person like you doesn't fight with a person because she feels like it. It's a forced situation. Even if I reveal the person's name to whom you're going to lose, you won't be able to resist yourself from not fighting. And can you save a person from death? It is not possible to love a person for 24 hours, as we believe we would do if we had a chance to go back. What you can do is apologise, because mistakes are relatively few. Now, while you apologise, try to make it as proper as possible. By proper, I mean that you should feel sorry on the inside. He is a simple person. He forgives easily and forgets. Because we're all somewhat the same, you must become a simple person too. He'd appreciate it very much. What other things can I tell you about? Tips and tricks? Well, I am ultimately an advanced version of you, so you better make mistakes, lest I will not reach this near-perfection without them.

Hence, this leads me to the ending here, but the last reminder, please. In the beginning, I mentioned a pandemic a couple of times. Didn't I? You don't need to worry about any of your acquaintances,

though. It didn't have much of an impact on your introverted and boring life. But a Delli-wale Mausa of your friend that you'll meet during post-graduation, named Kritika will, unfortunately, catch this virus. By nature's grace, he is saved, but if you think you can make them aware of the future COVID vaccines without leaving an eccentric impression, they might be saved from a miserable period. I put the word, you are smart enough to make your own decisions.

I'll try to write to you again. Maybe five years later? LOL. Feel free to send me your email if you ever wish to tell me what you expect from me. I know it's hectic to write. But hey, I'll be more than happy to hear that.

Putul Mangni Mandal

From a slightly wiser and older you.

Gauri Shukla

Gauri Shukla is a third-year Literature student pursuing her passion for reading and writing from the University of Delhi. President of the Literary Society of the college, she is an avid reader who yearns to get lost in estranged, galvanic worlds of art. A national-level debater, she is someone who doesn't shy away from speaking her mind. An ardent scripturient, she has written articles for The Times of India, The Hindu, The Redstockings Chronicles, etc. She's currently working on a South-Asian anthology as an editor alongside editors from Bangladesh and Pakistan. Her main interests of study lie in Diasporic postcolonial and African- American literature. She wishes to document the experiences and sentiments of different people, belonging to different cultures, all around the world. She believes life is too short and time is fleeting thus, each moment needs to be savored and felt to its optimum level. She likes to describe herself as a wandering cloud that romances with the sky, lost yet free.

CHAPTER FOUR

Letter 4

Dear Gauri,

I am so jealous of you. You're happier than me. You're playing with Jenny, going on walks with her, petting her and reading out from your favourite novels to her. I can imagine her looking at you as you read in a soft, hushed tone as if the words coming out of your mouth are only meant for her; a secret between the two of you. I miss Jenny a lot. It's been four years since she died, and I still miss her the same way I did on the night we lost her. It's like a permanent hole punched in my chest. That little fur baby owns that part of my heart. She has claimed it and it will forever remain hers. Can you do me a favour? Please don't let her eat anything she's not supposed to eat. It'll mess up her liver. And don't ignore her after she ruins your novel. You can always get a new novel. I have three different editions of that novel today. They just sit on my desk like showpieces because I still pick up the torn, chewed edition that still has Jenny's bite marks on it. Don't ignore her when she whines about wanting to play outside. I know studies are important and you've always been very serious about them but take her to play outside. Run with her in the park and roll with her in the dirt and play hide-and-seek with her. Take better care of her health. And spend as much time with her as you can. You must take her out for a swim. And more car drives where she can enjoy the wind run through her floppy ears. Save her. Try your best to save her. I did try my best. But it was too late. I wish in some other alternate universe, my fifteen year old can make different decisions.

A lot has changed. A lot. Things you wouldn't have ever imagined will happen. You'll move to a different house. It will feel hostile at first, but then you'll gradually come to terms with it. It'll feel empty and cold but the room will eventually become your haven so don't get too upset when you take a look at your room. Be kinder to it and it will open its arms and engulf you in a big warm hug. It will rock you to sleep on days when sleep abandons you. It will make you feel safe when the world would be battling with a deadly virus. You'll fall in love with an amazing guy but you'll lose your best friend. It will mess you up but you'll come out of it stronger. You'll lose dadi[1] right before college. One day, she'll be there, sitting in the courtyard, making her world-famous pickles and the next day, she'll be gone. Her scent will linger in your mind for days. I still remember papa[2] clutching onto her sari like a lost child, crying for his mother to come back. For days, you'll dream about her and let the tears stain the covers of your pillow. Do you remember when dadi used to casually say, "Ek din hum bhi chale jayenge[3]" and I used to get so upset and scold her for talking like that? I guess she was right. Death will come knocking one day on each of our doors and we'll have no choice but to leave. If it makes you feel any better, she died peacefully, in her sleep, with a hint of a smile on her face.

Also, I request you to stop wasting our parents' money on those goddamned engineering coachings. You are not going to be an engineer. It's a waste of time and money. DON'T DO IT! Also, I wish I had the chance to switch to Humanities while in school. That would've helped me so much. But it's alright. Science made me clever. By the way, I'm studying English Literature right now. Surprised?

Also, I had a near-death experience while getting admission in the college. I read somewhere that life is no more than a funeral procession winding towards the grave, its small joys the flowers of funeral wreaths...but despite all of it, the mere stupid humans that we are, we are sanguine, hoping for a better future. I did the same. Thought I understood life and then came the mind boggling revelation as I began to find myself often lost in the labyrinth of life, trying to find my way out. It was around five in the morning on the eleventh of July. We were on the Agra Lucknow Expressway, on our way to Delhi. Papa was behind the wheel. I had a car accident. My closest encounter with death. I couldn't move. I felt an intense burning sensation in my head. I was fully conscious but paralysed . My head wouldn't move . It was trapped between the front and back seat and I lay there twisted like a disfigured body. When I opened my eyes , I saw my parents, standing motionless like a tree. They stood glued to their spots, terror etched in their faces as they saw my twisted body thinking I was dead. That face, I will never forget that face. That's what death does to you. It suddenly takes away everything you loved and tosses it away into nothingness. I saw my father cry again. He kept apologizing, begging God to take him rather than me. I wanted to say that it was okay. That I was ...or would be okay. I wanted to soothe him but I lay motionless. And then I was blinded because of the immense flow of blood from my head. Got plastic surgery. Thirty seven stitches on my face, Sixteen stitches on my head and Seven stitches behind my left ear. The surgery went on for five hours, I was kept in the ICU, I had lost one heck amount of blood. Recovered yet lost.

The first few months of college won't be easy at all. You will feel out of place,homesick and depressed. But you'll eventually fall in love with the place and its people. You'll fall in love with the city of Delhi and the perfume emanating from its streets, your ears will get used to the buzz and the hullabaloo sizzling in the city so much so that Kanpur will feel very pallid and uneventful. You'll find amazing people in college. They won't judge you or stare at you for too long for having accident marks on your face. They won't make you feel uncomfortable about the way you look. You'll love the hostel even more than the college. You'll also get into fights but they'll only end up getting you closer to people. You'll drink beer for the first time and absolutely hate it. You'll make maggi at three in the morning. You'll experience a whirlpool of emotions and sometimes when you think you're going to drown, you'll come up onto the surface to breathe again and continue the struggle until you become powerful enough to face it head-on. This reminds me of the words of one of my professors in college. In the very first semester, she had said that college is not just about studies or having fun. It's that place where we get ready for the world. We gear up to embark upon new expeditions. We learn to challenge our inhibitions and truly figure out who we really are. And we meet people that hold our hands till the end. She was right. I might be lost but I know who I am and what I stand up for. I am not scared anymore to voice out my opinions or speak aloud of the things that need to be talked about. I am not the shy, silent kid anymore. A feminist through and through.

I still have a lot of internal demons to fight with though. I am trying to make things easy for you. Fighting constantly to be a better version of myself. This constant urge to create a masterpiece at the very first try, this constant habit of making simple things and ideas more complicated...I am tired! Always trying to be the best, the kindest, the perfect friend, the perfect student, the perfect child. Am I an attention-seeker? Somebody who likes to hog attention? Honestly, I don't know. This is all so confusing! Why can't I keep things simple and plain as they really are? In my constant attempt to make things complex, I fail to enjoy the process. I am a good person and capable of great things, I know that deep down. It's buried in my bones. I've got great potential. The only thing stopping me is my own self. This constant rat race that I'm running in, limping at this point, has dried up life for me; extricated it of all its beautiful juices that used to make me smile all the time. Now, I've got assignments to do. Following which, I've got more assignments to do. The never ending saga of college assignments, which would've been tolerable had I actually been in college!

Oh! I missed the part about the pandemic. At the start of my second semester in college, a deadly strain of the coronavirus, known as Covid-19, began to make rounds all around the world. Yes, you will be witnessing a pandemic, a pandemic that leads to a global shutdown. You'll be cooped up in your home for months. The deadly virus will visit your house as well. Hopefully, everyone will be fine and you'll think the worst has gone. But then the second wave will hit the world and it will crumble India to pieces. Mum and dad will get calls in the middle of the night, at four in the morning; you'll know someone close has succumbed to the fatal virus. People will fall like dominoes around you, each caught in the deadly maze of the Covid-19. The world will have transitioned into an online mode and after a while, college will become a distant memory that will only lead to a heavy sigh coming out of your mouth. I am even sighing while writing this right now. I read a poem by Thomas Hardy a few days back and it hit a raw nerve making me agitatedly vulnerable. It goes like this:

"I heard a small sad sound,
And stood a while among the tombs around:
'Wherefore, old friends,' said I, 'are you distrest,
Now, screened from life's unrest?'
----O not at being here:
But that our future second death is near;
When, with the living, memory of us numbs,
And blank oblivion comes!'"

A haunting story about a man who heard voices beneath tombs, voices bemoaning "a second death" when memories of the buried soul fade and oblivion awaits. And this hit me so hard. Oblivion scares me. Dying is one thing. But what happens when your memories of living in the real world begin to fade away? I want to be remembered. I want to be remembered and I want my memories to bring a smile upon the faces of people who remember me. I often wonder if I am a damaged person, floating like mercury, moving yet static. This is not a world of damaged people though. Nobody likes damaged people, let alone dare to love them. So, I put up a facade of a person who is ambitious, optimistic, and happy. The only thing is, I don't know for how long I'll be able to carry the weight of this mask. It's too much work and I feel tired. But will I be able to survive without the facade? Will anybody understand the real me? I don't know. I'll carry it till I wear off or till it wears off.

Love-it's complicated. Or maybe, I'm complicating a simple thing again. I don't know. But the thing I will never admit to anyone who's met me is how desperately I want to be loved, I don't think I could say it. How I want someone to hold my wrists and kiss my palms and smile at me, and want me, I want to be wanted and I don't know how long poetry or songs will substitute for being wanted.

In spite of all the things I've complained about in the previous paragraphs, I am doing my best to find my purpose and path, to find the real me and I will continue to do so because I've got dreams. And no matter what, I won't stop until I've fought for it rigorously. Also, I don't want to disappoint you. As I write this letter, I hope that in the alternate universe of our realities, the fifteen-year-old me is enjoying life and breathing in the scent of the present because the twenty-year-old me will be dwelling in the future a lot. But, I'll try enjoying the present more now. Maybe I'll go for a walk today. The weather is beautiful here. The crisp auburn leaves and the chills in the air are enough to ignite excitement in my little heart. I guess some things never change. I'll always be a winter child.

Gauri

A slightly wiser and older you.

Nishtha Trehan

Nishtha Trehan is a nineteen-year-old student at Atma Ram Sanatan Dharma College, University of Delhi, studying English Honours. In her breaks, she likes to read, write, and journal. This letter is written to her fourteen-year-old self in the hope that it resonates with all of you.

CHAPTER FIVE

Letter 5

Dear Nishtha,

It's Okay to Put Yourself First

To the girl who feels misunderstood by her parents, for that girl who can't get rid of her mood swings and keeps pissing everyone off, for the one who cries herself to sleep because her grades just aren't good enough, the one who is struggling with self-love, it is going to turn out okay. You must be doing your homework right now, mentally preparing yourself to ignore the snickers of the boys in your class who point at you and mock you, calling you a nerd. Or you might be trying to have your dinner in peace, only to listen silently as your parents argue and hurl insults at each other for the fifth time today. You might also be standing in front of the mirror, staring at your reflection in self-doubt... and repulsion. Your anemic, iron-deficient pallor flinches; your fingers running over the recent acne breakout as you try to smile with your crooked teeth. You remove your hairband and run your fingers through the frizzy mess you refer to as your hair, attempting to forget the harsh words of your family members about yourself.

I know you're occupied while studying the whole day because you don't have any other option. I know the pressure our mother has put on us since you were a child is overwhelming and it suffocates you. I know you feel trapped in a cage with no freedom to go out, to talk to your friends, or even read novels in peace. You don't get to do what you like or have any say in anything, but here I am, telling you that it gets better. I know how stubborn you are and how you've always hated listening to advice even though you give the best ones (sadly, your stubbornness is still irredeemable), but you're going to want to listen to my advice because I'm just like you, but older.

I'm who you never imagined being but would be immensely proud of. I know it sounds absurd, but everything you are experiencing right now will shape you in the future into the kind and empathetic person you have always secretly wished to be. The pain you feel right now will teach you how to control your emotions and be in control. I believe in you and guess what? These grades you worry about and will continue to worry about until you pass out of high school, do not matter. Repeat after me: they do not matter. You're not superior if you meet your standards, nor are you inferior if you do not do so. It's okay to breathe and to take a moment for yourself where you stop worrying all the time. Know that your body has a limit and always let yourself take a breather. The number of times you have gotten unwell over studies is self-deprecating and very unhealthy. Know and listen to your body's warning signs. Stop, rest, heal before beginning again.

You will learn what happiness is – you will fail first and make a lot of mistakes, but the lessons you will learn will teach you to love yourself inexorably. You will take care of yourself, put yourself first, and stop burning yourself for the sake of others. My girl, I'm not saying that you aren't going to have bad days because the concept of substantial happiness does not exist, but as long as you are there for yourself, you will be okay. So, discard your fear of disappointing your parents and, instead of trying to get good grades, try to learn. Seek knowledge wherever you go; it'll enrich your life. Because if you don't, you'll spend two years studying science, a subject you loathe, just to please your parents, which is impossible. Stop trying to please those who can never be satisfied. Therefore, I implore you to choose wisely. Choose what you want, but not at the cost of yourself and your self-respect. There will be moments ahead where you will feel overwhelmed and be tempted to make reckless decisions that would harm your relationship with the person most important in the whole world: you. So, do not forget to ponder first because you are incredibly strong and you should never let anyone do anything to make you feel weak.

As you grow, it is important to understand that you cannot save all relationships. Stop trying to! Those who care about you will always be there, and instead of being upset over those you've lost, focus on those who are always by your side. All you have to do is have faith in yourself and do what you love. I know being alone is terrifying, but is it really better to give yourself to people who wouldn't do the same for you? Instead, take a stand for yourself, say that you deserve better and mean it, take time to understand and sort yourself out, and treat yourself as an equal before finding people who will treat you as one too. Take up space and don't be afraid of putting yourself out. So, what if you get judged? Everyone gets judged a little bit every day anyway. I know you're currently rolling your eyes at this letter, but when you read it again after a few years, you will understand.

I want to tell you all the sadness inside of you that you can't seem to grasp and keep cursing yourself for, asking where it comes from? It's okay. You're fourteen and think you're a terrible person, but you're not. You're just a teenager whose body is changing, and that is affecting you. But you're yet to see the world. You've yet to experience so much of what is unprecedented to you right now. It is inevitable, then, that your perception of yourself will change. So, please understand that it is okay to not understand your feelings and thoughts as they do not define you. They will never define you, not until you give them the power to do so. Take back the power and you'll see what you've been missing. I know everything might seem scary, but that is okay. Take everything one step at a time. Live. Hold on to little moments of joy; they complete you. Do not just exist.

Talk to someone when you're having a bad day. Talk as much as you can. You can vent to friends, family, or anyone else who will listen. Stop keeping everything inside of you all the time. You're only doing more harm to yourself. In fact, talk to your mother; don't shut her out. I know you resent her and you might hate me for writing this, but she loves you and is doing everything to protect you. It's just that her love language doesn't coincide with yours. The day you both start understanding each other, it'll all get better. But you have to forgive her first and also forgive yourself for thinking that you're a terrible daughter. It's not true. You're both just humans mirroring the same grief, tiptoeing around each other, always trying to take each other's space.

I also want you to forgive me for putting you through everything that you are currently suffering from. I did not know any better back then. Unfortunately, for some, maturity comes with age, and you are exactly that. You are the person who learns from mistakes, refusing to even listen to any guidance that benefits you. But know this, the past doesn't define you nor does it make up your future because you are going to get so many opportunities in the future to change for the better.

Do not let go of your passion for art. Create as much as you can. Read as much as you can. Write, write, write, because these are the things that define you. You are you today because of the words you have read. Don't let society tell you otherwise. Neither should you ever let go of hope, because trust me, soon you are going to be in a place where you will think back on this and be so proud of yourself for never giving up on your art. Your hobbies, the music you listen to, the shows you watch, and the books you read influence you intrinsically and are part of who you are. They matter.

You will get through the days that worry you, the weeks that make you anxious, and the months that terrify you. Now take a second to be proud of yourself for everything you've achieved. I will always be your biggest supporter, and I understand if you do not take this letter seriously. As long as you realise that it is okay to put yourself first, my purpose here has been achieved. Before I bid you goodbye, imagine that I am giving you a warm hug, holding you so tight that all your broken pieces mend. Shh, it's okay to cry because I'll be crying with you. Just like how I'll be smiling along every time you are happy. Now promise me to reward yourself for each achievement.

A bucket load of love for you.

Nishtha

A slightly wiser and older you.

Raman Singh

Raman Singh was born in the year 2001 in Haryana, India. He never did things to pass time, when he held on to a thing, he gave himself completely to it. May it be playing basketball for nine years, may it be doing theatre, which also induced interest in literature. He is currently pursuing BA(Hons) in English, from Delhi University, and is an important part of the theatre society. He has also acted in six theatrical productions and has written several short plays and stories. Not to forget his love for Hindi Literature, which has added new dimensions to his imaginations and in which he finds those values and thoughts which otherwise would've been too late to discover. If there is anything else that he loves, that is a cup of coffee. His notion of feeling content and happy is to have A cup of coffee with a brownie while reading a book.

CHAPTER SIX

Letter 6

Dear Raman,

Don't be afraid to pick up this letter and read it. I know you're not so adventurous. But don't be frightened by this letter. This letter comes to you from the future. And who doesn't want to know about their future? Now, if you have picked up the letter, I should inform you that it is your five-year-old self writing to you. And the best part is that you have changed a lot. Drastically. You would never have thought you would become someone who would read books and do theatre. The theatre has played a major part in changing you. It would introduce you to many people. It would open you. Your brain would think more. Your fear... Fear, I remember that you could not score a basket if someone came towards you. But you know what, this five-year-old Raman would do that easily. He is not frightened of people anymore. He has finally gained that confidence. You have. You would be proud of yourself. The other thing that theatre did for you was give you your feelings, those emotions that you might not have discovered. But there were some special people in the theatre who would do that. It helps you discern emotions. They will always have a special place in your heart. Especially KANK (you will get to know her).

Let's move on to books. My boy, you will be in love with them. You'd become the avid reader that you'd never been in your class.But don't worry, you will become one. Books would be loved by you. And by the way, you will be studying English literature. Literature has been the work of the theatre. Just never leave Theatre. It has worked wonders for you and will keep on doing that. And, yes, you would be doing a lot of great things. By this time, you would have worked in six productions. By the way, the seventh is the day after tomorrow. You would not only read, but write too. You would write poetry, stories, and plays. And I know you will explore more.

The other thing is Raman, I know, at this stage you don't have any friends. And you would not have till the school ends. But you know what, not having friends is something you would always wish for but would never have. The best part is that in those years, you would not be thinking about this much. To you, this would be normal. As you progress in the theatre, this thing will hit you more. Not to say that you will be sad or depressed, but you will be conscious of it. But books would become your friends. You will be taking them with you wherever you go. Irrespective of whether you get time to read them or not, they will travel with you.

Another thing I would say is that you are a good person. True person. Honest person. Keep that thing up. Did you ever think that you would be distracted by a couple sitting near you? Sorry to break this chain, as I was saying to keep the good things you have. They will make you; they will be your defining factors. Never leave them.

Now let us come back to basketball. By this time, you would have known that you didn't pursue basketball. You will leave this two and a half years later and join the theatre. But you know, this game would shape you too. All those people you would be hearing from said things that would come back to you many years later. And you would laugh at them. You'll remember everything your Coach said to you. They would also help you. All I want to say is that what you will be doing with your life will be beneficial to you and shape you, particularly through theater.

If there were books, then how could there not be coffee? You will love coffee. This is the thing about you, anything that comes into contact with you or that you start doing, you love that thing. This is something I am living these days. This is how you prove the meaning of your name. You would always have love to give to others. Because you never had friends, there was always love stored inside you. But do not worry you will get things to vent it out on. Books, coffee, theatre, and people.

Now, the other thing is that don't think much. I think a lot. Sometimes I overthink. You don't. This thinking is the gift of the theatre, but then use it when you write, not when you just ponder over things. It would be of no good. You will do some things that I can't tell you about in advance. Because you get to them too. Or else you would be not what you are right now. But then after doing them, don't think much. They were a part of this journey. Journey of growing up. You will discern a side of you that you never thought you had. But be happy about it.

There would be some things that you would do and then regret doing. But don't worry, they will not trouble you much. Again, thanks to you for reading the books.

Now in the theatre, you will meet people with whom you will attach yourselves with. But the twist would be that you would not even know about it. You will find yourself crying when those people would go away from you. This is the gift theatre would give. I know I am repeating this, but the fact is that you will remember those days. These days will shape you. Theatre will shape you. What I am saying is that your life will change, you will change. You will like this change. Of course, this change will bring its own set of problems, but you will easily face them.

You know, the best part about this change is that the things that bother you now and those that will come later will be irrelevant to you.This is what happens. Life changes and those things we think about a lot become of zero importance. I have learned this, and I am telling you.

Another benefit of theatre is the ability to express yourself.Finally, you will be able to share your emotions and express them. At first, it will take time, but slowly, as you delve into books, you will grow, and your mind will grow. It would be a wonderful thing.

You will be different, Raman. You were always. You were not meant to be like others. You would do things that no one could and would not do. Should I say that because you will become an artist and will be immersed in artistic things, you will be different? I can say so. This art will build you up.

Life will introduce you to things you never imagined. So, what do you think? That doesn't happen. It could never happen. Because if what you thought started happening, then you find yourself in ruins. These days, I overthink a lot of things. You don't. Keep it cool. Don't trouble yourselves with stupid thoughts. They are of no use. One thing I am jealous of about you is that you don't think much. I know you didn't know a lot of things, but at least you were saved from thinking much. Don't let any insecurities waste your time, as they do mine. Whenever any thought like that comes, read this letter, and assure yourself that what is scaring you today won't be of any importance. This is how life works. Therefore, believe in this process of growing up.

Many great things are waiting to come to you, and they will come at exactly the right time. Many things will upset you too. But today, as I write this letter, I am happy that those things occurred. I would have been something else if any one of those hadn't occurred. Some of them will disturb you a lot. I will not leave you. But you will be strong enough to face them. And yes, a very special person awaits you in your first year of college. That person will change your life. Will help you grow more. That person will introduce you to more new things and add new experiences to your list. You will love her.

In the end, I would say that right now I am sitting in a café that you once visited at five in the morning. which gives you a different level of peace. I am sitting here, this letter was given to me as an assignment, and I have been doing it for the past two hours. Again, this is the thing I love about you and me—we don't leave things midway. We don't do things to pass the time. When we start doing something, we completely devote ourselves to it. So, live your life. Don't think much. Great things await you.

Raman

From a slightly wiser and older you

Khushi Kaushik

Khushi Kaushik, the elder child in a nuclear family, was born and brought up in Faridabad, Haryana. She studied in DAV public school, sec 14, Faridabad, and was good in studies since childhood. She had a keen interest in studying literature. The author of 'Secret of room 333' is known for her flash fiction. She started writing her first book when she was 13, which is a very young age, her interest developed in the field of content writing and she started to write poems , stories and finally decided to write a fiction . She is 20 at present and is pursuing English literature from University of Delhi. Apart from being an author she is a poetess as well and her compilation of romantic poems 'Shades of love' had a great readership. She is an eager learner and has various interests. She has a keen interest in art, she has been painting since childhood and is a very good singer as well and also has won competitions in singing . She has a dynamic personality and is someone who loves to take up new challenges and broaden her horizons.

CHAPTER SEVEN

Letter 7

Dear Khushi,

I know you are brave and confident that you have it all figured out. But let me tell you, you are still naive. You have a lot to see and a lot to learn. Do not let your guards down. Five years from now,

you will sit here and regret it. I know he left you. I know how devastated you are, but don't take desperate steps to get him back. Because if you do, you will lose your dignity. You will be approached by many guys, don't pay heed. Don't think they are your friends. They will come, see your flaws, show pity to get you, and once they get what they want from you, they will leave you shattered and more broken with more scars to live with.

You are with everything that is beautiful in this world. You are way too rare for them to become too common. Don't just play hard to get, be hard to get. Just run away from all of those dicks as fast as you can so that they can never hurt you. No, don't let that guy across the street come over. You think he is nice and all, but he is going to come in and leave you broken in just 10 minutes. You wouldn't even know what happened. And by the time you realise it, it will be too late. So just don't let him see you or even talk to you. Stay away from the guys who are full of lust. They are incapable of giving you what you desire. It's a waste of time. I know you are desperate for love because your first long-term relationship ended, but don't be so desperate to settle halfway.

You deserve it as a whole, not in bits and pieces. Don't change yourself. Be the jolly person you are. Don't try to be the bitch you are not. I am telling you it will take you a long time to recover and discover who you are. Fill in the form for Jesus and Mary you will get in under your desired course. I don't want you to cry later if only you had not filled out the form.

Don't waste your precious first year in the drama people are causing. Enjoy yourself but stay out of drama, or else you will also be a prop for them. Don't waste your time out there sitting in a park, traveling, and discovering Delhi instead of waiting for his text or call. Go out and live a little for yourself. Years later, you will get a chance to meet your old friend after 12 years, don't miss it because you want to go to a party. Meet him. He's not going to come again for ages. Embrace the moment before he's gone back and you regret not having met him.

But if you just want to tear this letter apart, which I know you will because you are stubborn and don't like to be told what to do, then it's fine too. Because if I were to do it again, I wouldn't change a thing. If I am this wise and mature today then it is because of all that I have been through. It is painful, heartbreaking, you will lose your dignity, self-respect, freedom, and a lot more, but that is how you shall grow. You can take the shortcut for now but then you wouldn't like the person you will be. You wouldn't be me. And I love the way I am with all my scars and flaws.

So do it all. Within a heartbeat. Everything comes and goes, and so will the love, and so will the pain. Fall and fail and get up. You will love many, but don't forget to {which I know you won't} love yourself.

Love.

Khushi

From a slightly wiser and older you .

Hoilalnei Hmar

Hoilalnei Hmar is a 21-year-old resilient struggler who juggles her movement between Manipur and Delhi often. At a young age, she had done several horrifying things. Her friends would not play with her; the reason is unknown. She revealed that it might be because of poverty or her parents' strictness. She was bullied by her own classmates and her neighbouring friends. Life was hard for her just like the rest of it will be. So, she decided to bestow courage to her own younger self and her present one. The courage that every one of us needs when we are treated differently by our own dear ones.

CHAPTER EIGHT

Letter 8

Dear Hoilalnei,

You are incredible. You make this world a little bit more wonderful. You have so much potential and so many things to do. You are doing amazing. You are doing well. You are incredible. So many people, even your best friends, tried to pull you down, but you know what? You are the best. No one is funnier than you. I'm so proud of what you have become and achieved today. No matter what people try to bring you down, just be yourself. You don't need boys to look or feel better. You are true when you are yourself. Life is also beautiful here, so you do not have to worry about what is going to happen to you in five or ten years. You do not need to find love just because your friends are finding one. The time will come for you too, and when the time comes, no omen on this earth can stop you two from becoming one. It doesn't matter what you have lost and found while trying to find yourself. People come and go, and the people who choose to stay are the real ones. Do not forsake them. Keep them close to your heart because "real is rare." Be with people who love and adore you and appreciate everything you do, not people who try to drag you down at any chance that they get. Stay away from people that don't make you feel secure about your body, your face, and even your complexion. They are not worth talking to. The only time you are going to enjoy it to the fullest is NOW, so spend every minute wisely in order to avoid regretting it in the future. No one is going to love you like you love yourself. The world is cruel out there. Even your dearest friend can be a snake. You never know when they will bite you. There is not only one snake but more than one. They gather and gossip about you, and make plans to bring and tear you down. This is what life is about. If your friends are happy with your success, keep them. They need you. You need them. They count on you.

Do what makes you happy, not what people decide is best for you. Start loving yourself by following a skincare routine, working out, and drinking more water. Do not forget to eat healthy, or you'll regret it when your tummy bulges out. Life is too short to whine about what you do not have. Instead, embrace what you have, and that will make you feel the safest and most confident in your life. You will make mistakes. Not just one, but several. Do not avoid that, but learn from it. You're a fool if you make the same mistakes twice. Be slow to judge and kind to everyone for you do not know that the happiest smile on the face can commit suicide by just one word that you told him being stuck on his head. Do what pleases you, but after you bring your own food to the table, not while mom and dad are doing it for you. Save more and spend less. You do not need them now, but you will need them later when the family financial crisis breaks out again. Do everything in the name of Jesus. Never forget to thank Him, and never enough, for what he has done for you is priceless. He was your guide, both now and until you left this sinful world. Love your parents and your brothers and sisters. Nobody will love you like they do, no matter who comes into or crosses your life. You were sent here on this earth for a purpose. The purpose of your life is to figure out WHO you really are and WHAT you came for.

There is a time here when I feel like going back there. There are also times that I wish things were different. I've always had this coming. So, don't do things that you are going to regret. You are not perfect. You have to accept yourself as you are, no matter how much people tell you to change. There are some that you have the potential to change, but some do not like your complexion. Feel alive when you are with someone who encourages you and has faith in you. They are the path to second happiness. The first thing is what I told you in the beginning, about yourself. No matter how many times life tries to knock you down, dust yourself off and get ready for the next ride. Keep this on repeat till you get what you want. If you fail, tell yourself it's okay and move on to the next level. Do not expect people to do good to you every time. Always be ready to face the worst in them. Life is unpredictable. Love and be kind to everyone you've come across. Trust me, you do not want to regret thinking over and over again about the negative things you've done to them. Be the best version of yourself at any time and anywhere. That's how you carry elegance. I'm so proud of what you've been through and where life is taking you. It's full of surprises. The you that's had a rough week. The you that seems to be under constant storm clouds. The you that feels invisible. The you that does not know how much longer you can hold on. The you that has lost faith. The you that always blames yourself for everything that goes wrong.

You have time. Better things are coming your way, so please hang in there. You can do it!

Live your life to the fullest.

Hoilalnei

A slightly older and wiser you.

Thank You!

Dear Reader,

Thank you for making it through this anthology. We, the other writers and I, appreciate you. We'd be thrilled if you had anything to contribute or if you had feedback on this collection. You can post it online or send it to us at swara@nrityanganakalakendra.com.

Swarnika

Printed by Libri Plureos GmbH in Hamburg,
Germany